Watercolor

Meet The Brushes

Create The Stroke and Control The Flow

By

Barbara A Parish

Writer and Illustrator

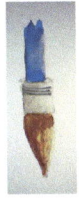 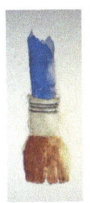 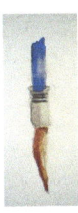 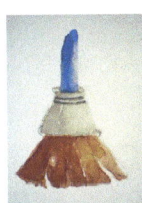 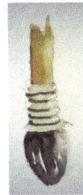

Barbara's Note

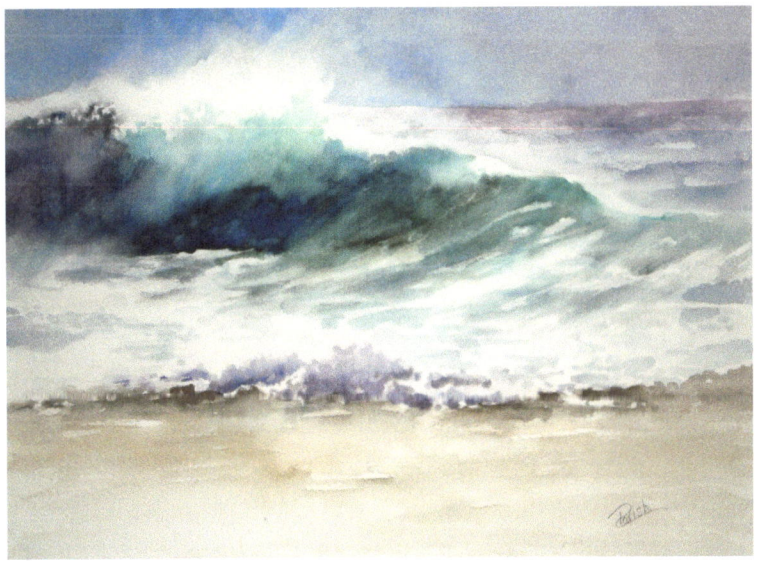

Surf's Up © Barbara Parish 2016

Introducing the most important tool in your painting gear.

The Watercolor Brush

- Did you know each brush is made to do a specific stroke?
- Did you know you have a choice on brush hair?
- Did you know cleanup is quick and easy?

You can master brush strokes by knowing which brush to use for a specific technique.

To learn a brush stroke, you need to read the words, see the stroke, and then practice until you master working with the brush. It's the same as learning a new language, hear the words, see the words, and speak the words.

Practice is the key!

So, learning to paint with watercolor will take every ounce of attention and motivation you can muster.

Desire ~ Tenacity ~ Practice

Helpful Hints:

1. Watercolor can be changed on the paper, erased, altered, and played with. Knowing this fact will help you relax while learning. No need to panic about doing it right the first time. That is, until you know what you are doing, and then you will strive to do the stroke right the first time.

2. The magic tool to lighten or remove color from watercolor paper is to use a baby TOOTHBRUSH. Yes, a baby size toothbrush with flat bristles. Wet the toothbrush; bring the water to the paper, gently brush the paper to release the color, and then blot with a paper towel.

3. Painting with a watercolor brush takes a delicate touch, water will discharge easily when pressure is applied.

4. Each brush is made to do a specific stroke. Your job is to know the strokes and practice. There is the word **PRACTICE** again.

A short story about my first watercolor workshop

I registered for a week workshop with a well-known watercolor artist, my destination, Crescent City. I was beyond excited, walking into class with a big smile, caring a new portfolio, new palette, new paints, and wonderful full sheets of watercolor paper. Yes, I was a beginner. I looked around for a seat, and then I spotted the teacher. She had her hand over her brow and muttered the words "Oh No"! That's when I understood her body language. I was in an intermediate skill level workshop where I didn't belong. I was a newbie.

The days went by, I learned so much watching her demonstrations, and trying new techniques. On the last workshop day, the assignment was to use a touch of Viridian Green into the face I was painting. I sat there frozen, I just could not pick up the green and drop that color into the face. The teacher came over and stood behind me waiting for me to do something! She smacked me on the shoulder with loving intention, saying **JUST DO IT!**

I was tickled, terrified, and just did it! I was so pleased with myself after the five-day workshop. I packed the car with a grin on my face, and drive back to Southern California, knowing watercolor was the medium for me to discover. I hope you will experience the same excitement and discovery that I have enjoyed for many years.

YOUR JOB!

Relax, and hold the brush loosely. Remember this is a gentle medium, no need to force a shape or value or color. It is up to you to understand the painting process and **PRACTICE**.

My Job!

I'll share my knowledge about watercolor brushes. I'll give you the encouragement to learn which brush to use for what technique, and learn how to care for your watercolor brushes.

This is your beginning! This book is filled with information about brush strokes and care. It's up to you to keep learning and developing your painting skill. Barbara

Dedication

I dedicate this book to my Friday Painters Class

Their tenacity and thirst for learning sparks my passion for teaching and writing about watercolor techniques, and the courage to paint.

Copyright

Table of Contents

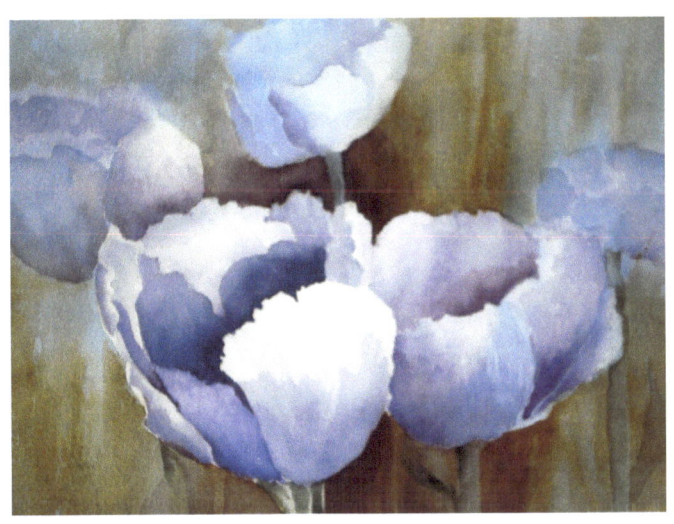

1

How To Handle A Watercolor Brush

Round   Flat   Rigger   Fan   Mop

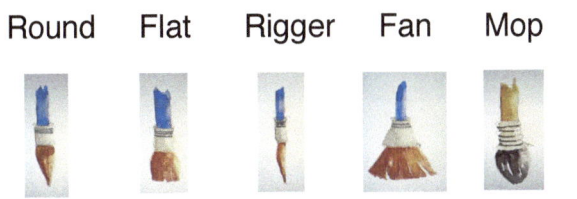

I chose to introduce five basic watercolor brushes,
These brushes will give you a good start with brush
knowledge and control.

The brush is an extension of your intension.
Everyone has individual flair when signing his or her

name. That same flair will show up in your brush stroke.

Brush Hair Type

Natural ~ Animal hair, Sable or Kolinsky, holds a large amount of water.

Brush spring-back is slight ~ press on wet brush and the hair doesn't spring-back to shape when lifted from the paper.

Blend ~ Natural hair blended with, Synthetic filament, holds a good amount of water, but not as much as the Natural Brush. Brush spring-back is medium.

Synthetic ~ Nylon man made filament, holds the least amount of water. Brush spring-back is instant.

Badger or Squirrel ~ Animal hair, holds enormous amount of water. Brush has no spring back. Wimpy!

Hold the watercolor brush at the end of handle, as shown below. The brush is a lightweight object with no resistance, so hold loosely. Another reason to hold the brush loosely in your hand is to move the color on paper and make interesting marks. The brush will work standing on its tip to draw a thin line, lay flat using more pressure to mark a wider stroke, or lay on its side and drag across paper to hit the high bumps of textured paper.

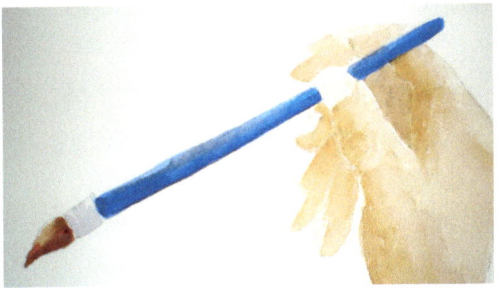

Avoid stroking the paper to fill-in an area. Stroking the paper many times in one area will ruin the luminosity of the white paper. Drag across paper one time, and then reload. Touch the edge of first stroke as you make another stroke. Try not to go back into the wet area, just touch the edge of a wet stroke and let the paint settle on its own. This will give you the best of color intensity and luminosity.

Brush clean up is simple! Swish the brush in clean

water and blot on a paper towel. Lay brush on flat surface to dry. Store vertical with brush hair up in attractive jar or lay in brush carrier with the brush hair free from pressure. If you care for your brushes they will last for years.

So, think and do! Stroke color on paper, lift brush off paper, reload your brush, and make another stroke next to and touching the edge of first stroke. Always rinse your brush before changing colors. Keep a clean water container next to you while painting.

These five brushes, and variety of strokes, will help you get started painting with watercolor. After you are comfortable using these brushes, look for the Novelty brushes that make fun strokes.

Practice is the key!

Now Let's Get Started!

Notes and Ideas

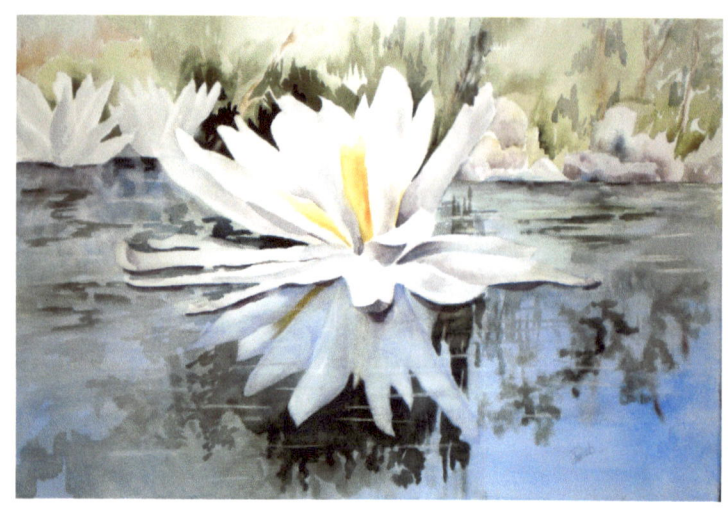

2

Round Brush

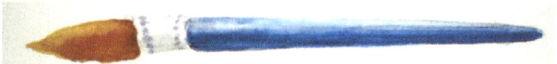

The Round brush is numbered to indicate size, ranging from very small to extra large. Starting with number 1 as small.

The fat belly of a round brush holds the watercolor. Pressure on the brush hair will discharge the watercolor. Light pressure on tip will make a thin line with a dryer stroke. Heavy pressure on tip will spread the brush hair and discharge a large amount of watercolor making a wide watery stroke.

This round brush is so versatile you might not think of changing brushes while painting. I suggest, when you know what strokes these five brushes can make, you change the brush type for the stroke you are striving for.

Working with the fat part of the brush, lay brush horizontal to the paper dragging the belly slow and deliberate, this will release paint in all the peeks and valleys of paper texture. A fast drag across the paper will touch color to the peeks leaving the valleys to show some white of the paper. This stroke has a funny name, Dry Brush.

Each watercolor brush has a shape designed to create a specific stroke. The bigger the brush the larger area the brush covers.

The belly of the brush holds the water like a reservoir, controlled pressure will regulate how much color will be released.

A loaded brush moving fast across dry paper will give the sense of sparkle on paper.

The speed of the swipe determines how many valleys are left without paint, to give the illusion of sparkle. See the sparkle on right side of the brush?

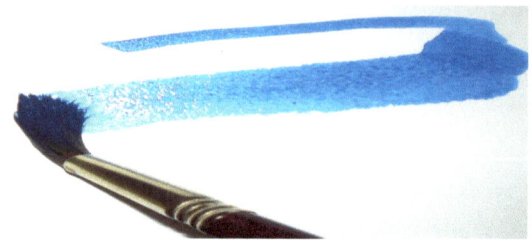

Start with a thin line, using slow stroke with light pressure. Change to medium pressure for a wide shape, using a fast stroke to the left will skip over the valleys of the paper. This technique used for glints of sun light or moonlight on water, rough wood, glints on a wet street, etc.

Practice will be the key to learning the strokes and how to use the right amount of water in your brush. Oh, I don't want you to think this is difficult, but it takes practice! So, chunk it down, I believe step-by-step learning will give you a good foundation of knowledge and easy recall to enjoy painting with watercolor.

In example, hold the brush vertical to the paper, with light pressure the brush tip will mark the paper with a thin line, more pressure the brush lays down giving a wider stroke. This pressure technique to control the flow of water from the brush can be used with all brushes.

If I had one brush choice to start my adventure with watercolor, it would be a round brush #8.

A variety of strokes can be made with the round brush.

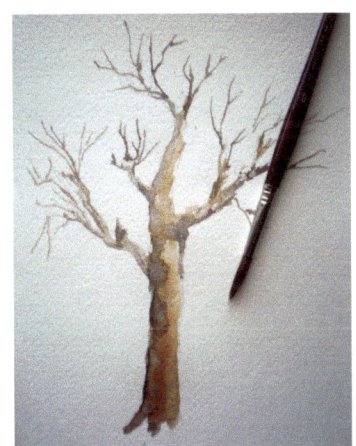

The tree trunk below is wide, so use the full width of brush to drag color up the trunk to the limbs.

Hold brush, vertical, up on tip, using less pressure to

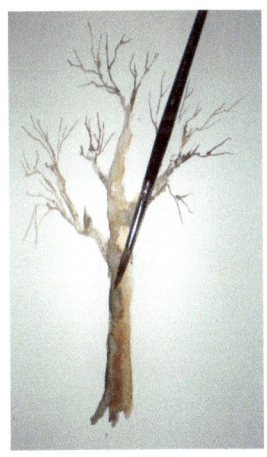

paint the limbs.

Technique Vocabulary:

Mingle or Merge of Color

Mingle: Color puddle touches another puddle to blend edges. This is a great technique to show how one color touching another creates a soft edge showing a third color.

Merge: Wet color dropped into another wet color, causes paint to move away allowing the new color to have its own shape.

Bloom or Blossom

Touching wet color to damp color will cause an irregular edge. The damp paint absorbs the wet paint causing edges that look like a bloom. Works for me!

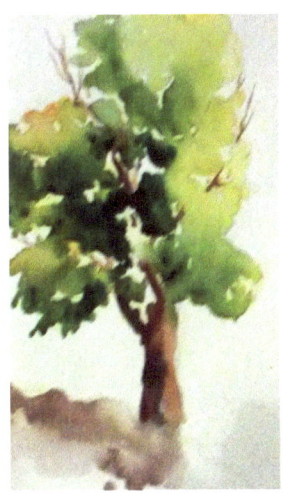

Touch the wet edge of yellow with a yellow green color, rinse brush, load dark green, and touch the wet edge of the yellow green puddle. This will show a beautiful mingle and merge look, with no hard edges, but lots of color. This technique eliminates the puzzle piece look of hard edges. Don't you agree?

Try not to stay inside a sketched shape when placing color on paper. Avoid painting the look of a puzzle, piece after piece. Let the brush move with wet color on the paper. Rinse your brush, pick up another color, touching the wet edge of first color. This causes the color to mingle and merge.

The above example you can see how gorgeous these colors look when free from edges. The color interaction is fresh and exciting, not dull looking and overworked.

Notes and Ideas

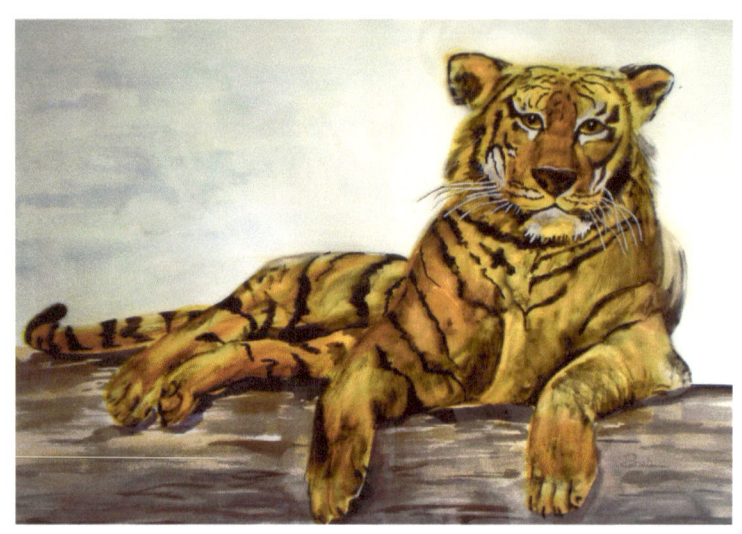

3

Flat Brush

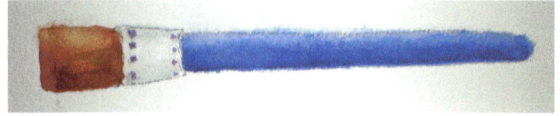

Chiseled edge, fat belly, and corners

If I had one choice for a flat brush it would be a 3/4 flat. The flat design allows a wide stroke that will turn into a thin line by twisting and lightening the pressure as the brush lifts up on chiseled edge.

Also try a double load, one color on the right corner and another color on the left corner. The water will blend colors when pressure is applied to brush.

Below is how to hold a flat brush to perform a stroke.

- Straight up on chiseled edge
- Diagonal to use brush sides
- Horizontal using brush belly

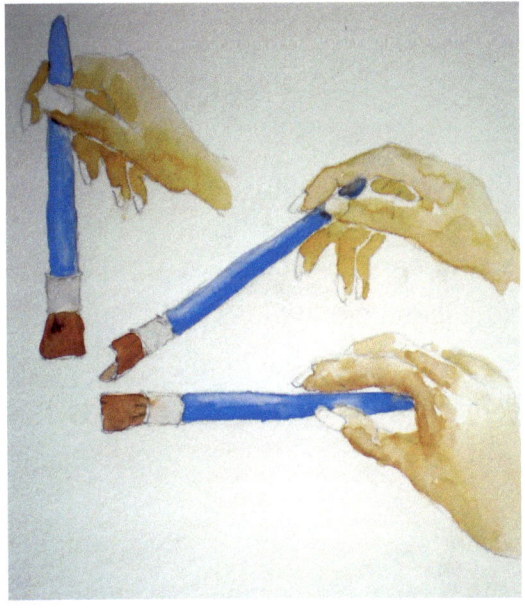

Below is a good example of using brush pressure to accomplish a specific stroke.

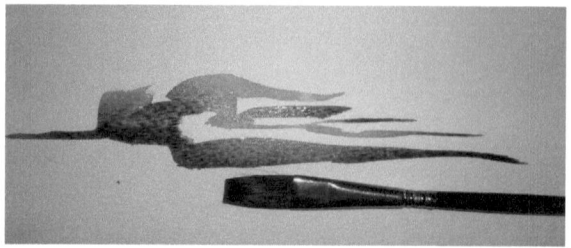

* A thin line leads using the chiseled edge of brush.

* Twist the brush to the wide side using pressure. This widens the stroke.

* Lessen the pressure and turn the brush up on it chiseled edge to make a thin stroke.

This is one long continuous stroke with surprises along the way like: color, value, and shape changes. Practice this stroke. The information on color value will be explained in my next book, Value to Color Parallel.

Now, pick up a brush and start practicing a stroke. Remember that each brush has a different stroke to learn and experiment with.

The brush image below is on its side showing the narrow part of the brush. The Flat brush will drag, swipe, and push, wide washes and glazes.

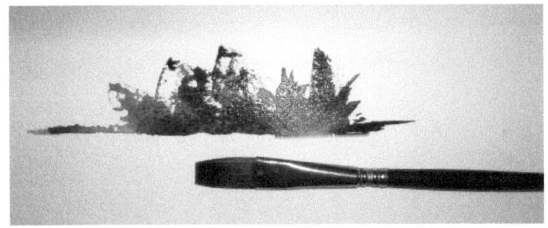

- Washes fill large areas with color.
- Merge another color by touching the edge of first wash; this is a very attractive stroke.
- Glazes are one wash of color, let dry, and then wash another color over the dry color. Use one stroke to avoid disturbing the first dry color.

Above the brush is shown on its side, hold horizontal to the paper, touch paper pushing up and lift.

Remember with every stroke put your own personality into that stroke. This is one of the reasons I say don't sit and paint all the time. Stand, think on your feet, and be free with the brush stroke. Standing at the easel, extending your elbow, allows your brush to show painterly strokes.

See the irregular stroke examples below.

Start the stroke with the flat of the brush, turn the brush up on its chiseled edge, and back to the flat brush for an irregular stroke. Use various combinations of this stroke.

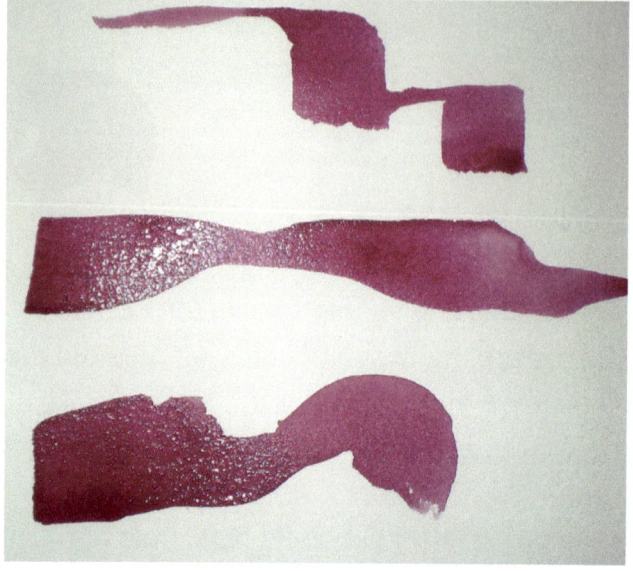

* To eliminate the dry hard edge, wet and wiggle brush to soften edge.

Notes and Ideas

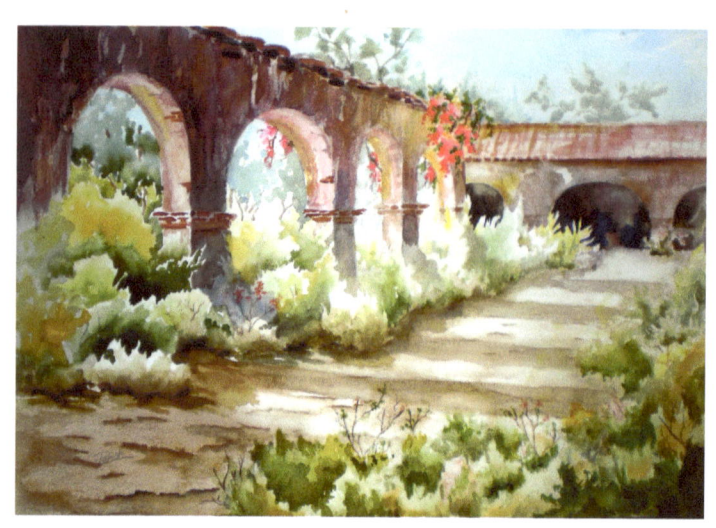

4

Rigger Brush

Small, Medium, Large, long thin hair with point

The rigger brush manages all the small accent lines and marks, wire, telephone lines, brush, tall grasses, tree tranches, palm fronds, etc.

If I had one choice for a Rigger, I would use a #5

Hold loosely at end of handle to flip and drag for lines and marks on the paper. You might feel out of control at first, keep practicing, you will see how this technique will give your painting fresh unstructured strokes. Painting the essence of a branch with a twitch in your stroke is the trick. At the

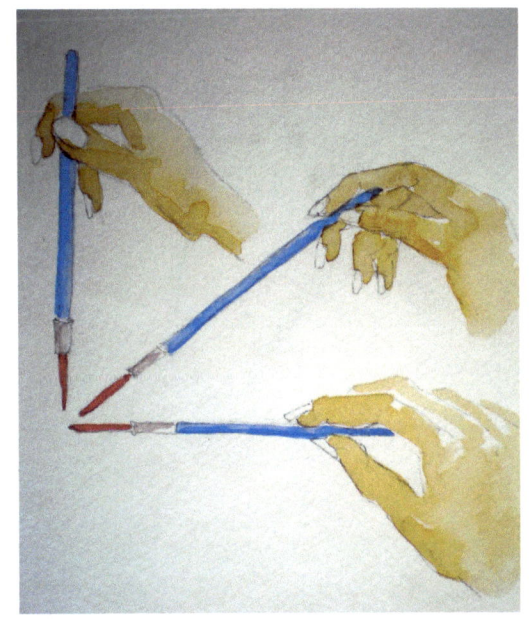

twitch, you will add a new branch. Building your tree brushes.

Below is the tree trunk painted with the #8 round brush. Now it's time to add the limbs and branches. That takes a more delicate touch for a thinner line.

Start the branches at the twitch bump in a limb, your connection point. Place rigger at twitch and flick out and away from the limb. This will vary the value of the branch and give it an uneven stroke.

Use the same type of stroke for the weeds shown below. Bring stroke from inside of bushes, up and away from the mass. Use the jerking method to add interest. Notice the weeds are NOT uniform they are irregular.

See the example of small branches at the end of tree limbs and ground weeds. This dormant tree shows the small branches.

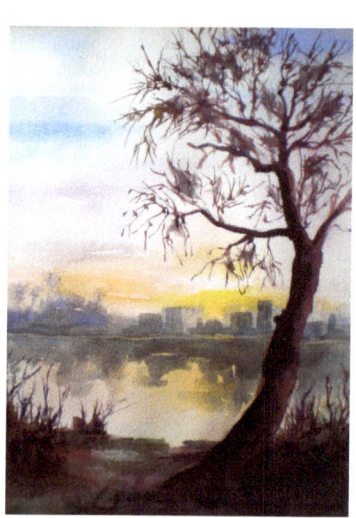

1. Load rigger
2. Place brush tip at a twitch spot to start another branch.
3. Drag and jerk as the stroke extends.
4. Add branches, think variety with every branch. Long, short, fat, thin, etc. Always make branches and limbs look different.

Notice the change in values on the tree trunk. Heavy pressure on brush discharges more color. Light pressure discharges less color. Pull over tree shape keeping continuous brush stroke on paper while adjusting the pressure. Then go back when dry and paint some areas again to darken or define. Remember the TWITCH or SHAKE in your stroke will add interest.

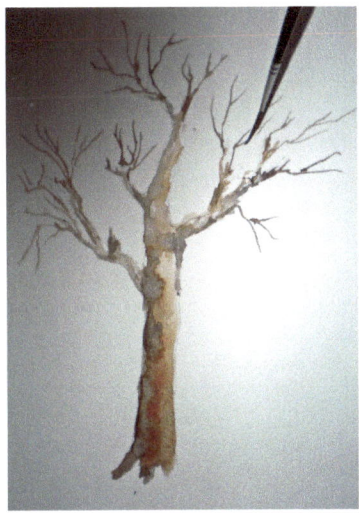

Example of brushes used in Demo:

• Rigger, ground shrubs and tree branches

• Round, limbs, trunks, sky, water, reflection

• Flat, city, water, clumps of grass

• Fan, all weeds

• Mop, washes of color

Notes and Ideas

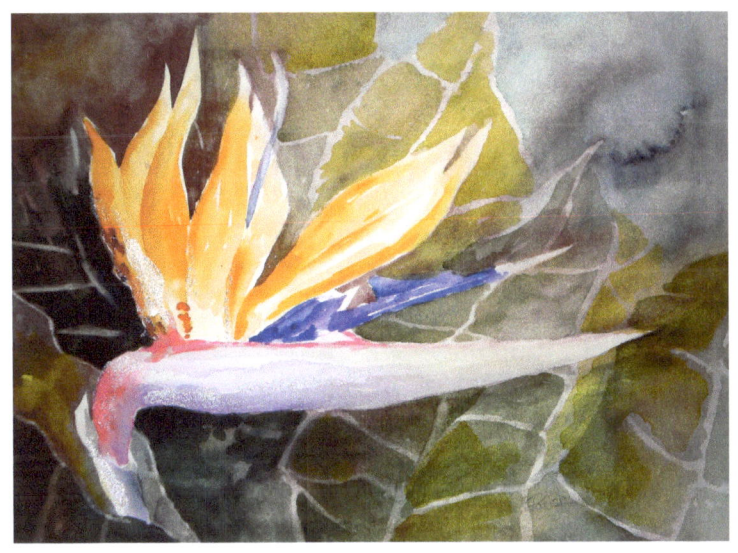

5

Fan Brush

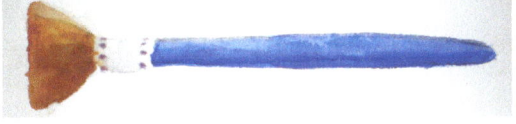

Small, Medium, and Large Fan shaped with chiseled edge

The Fan, use on chiseled edge and stroke thin broken line for palm fronds, limbs, and grasses. Lay on width and drag for textured lines used on siding, tree trunks, telephone poles, and fence posts. Use on edge and drag. If I had one choice for a fan brush I would choose #4.

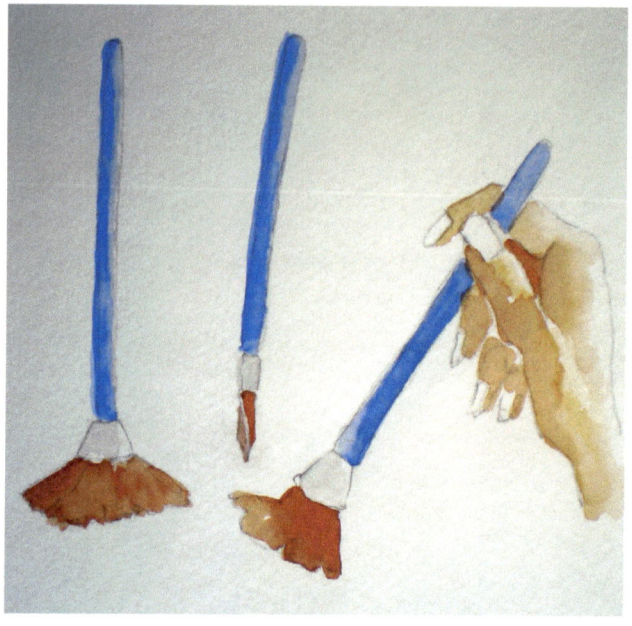

The Fan brush is perfect for what I call a broken stroke. Drag chiseled edge, lift off paper, and start to drag again, lift off paper, then flip to the right or left to make a wide stroke.

The Palm Fronds are a perfect subject for the Fan Brush. Paint the length of the spine with the edge of brush, put a jerk in your stroke as you extend the spine. This gives an irregularity to the stroke. This is called a painterly stroke. Then gently flip to the right or left of spine to form the palm. Holds plenty of color to do these creative strokes.

Remember that irregular shape of the palm fronds is very important. Over all, the tree must **not** look round.

I like to start my fronds with a light yellowish green, then stroke over with a medium green like Earthen Green. In the 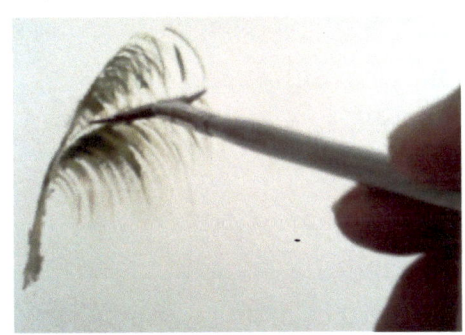 examples below, look for a subtle change in color. Hold the brush at handle end, extend brush to the paper to make a stroke. You will feel a little out of control and awkward, do it anyway. Repetition will improve the stroke. You are after painterly strokes, loose and free, allowing the brush to flip and drag at a whim.

Train yourself to paint expressive strokes, not just painting color inside the shape. This is where I 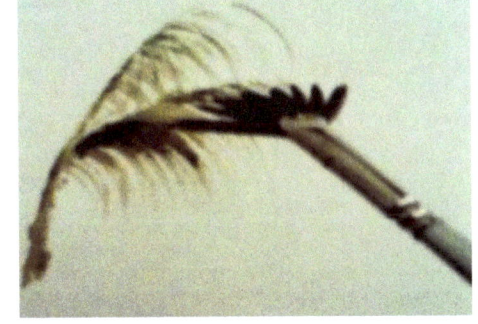 mentioned your personality would show in your stroke.

How you flip the brush, how you jerk the stroke, and how you lay down the paint with flair will develop your painting style.

The example shows what a Fan brush looks like when wet. This brush design enhances creative strokes.

See the openings in the frons, that stroke can work because of the splits in the hair. If the Fan brush didn't exist, the technique would be one stroke at a time with a Rigger brush.

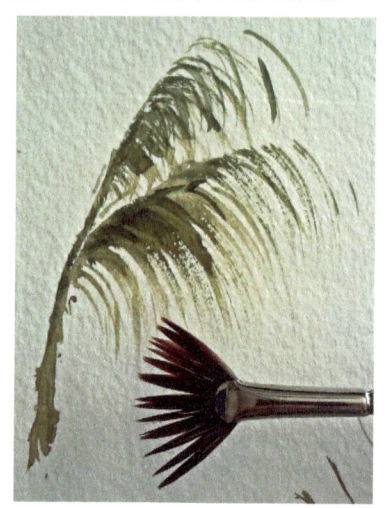

I use this brush for weeds, branches, fence wire, shadow shape, etc.

Notes and Ideas

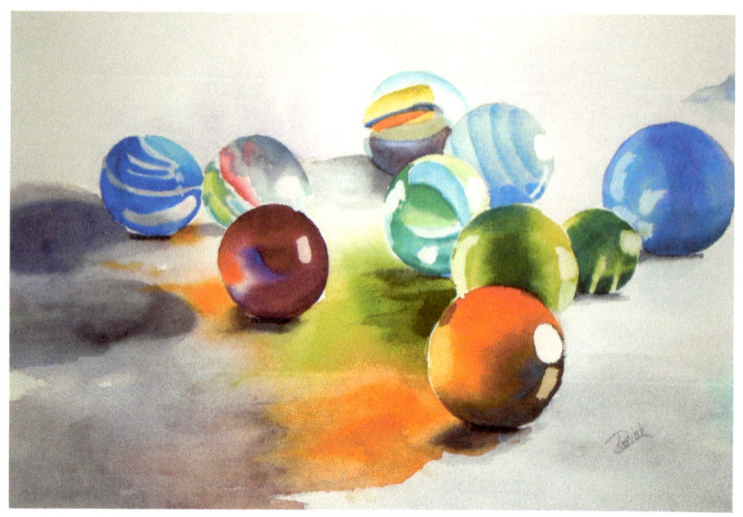

6

Mop Brush

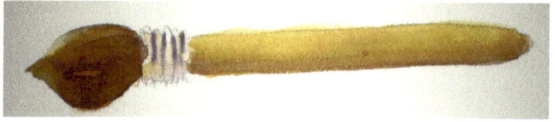

Small, Medium, and Large a thick round with point

The mop has thick hair in the furl wrapped in plastic with wire holding all together. Its wide belly will hold a large amount of water, and when wet sports a tip.

Lays down large amounts of water to perform long twists and turns or puddles of color. Used for the first wash to cover a large area.

Again, if I had one choice for a Mop, it would be a large mop. This brush holds a tremendous mount of water. The brush hair is limp with no spring. This is an advantage, making exciting marks on the paper or spreading water all over paper is perfect for the drop in color technique.

Large color washes can be your first step when starting a painting.

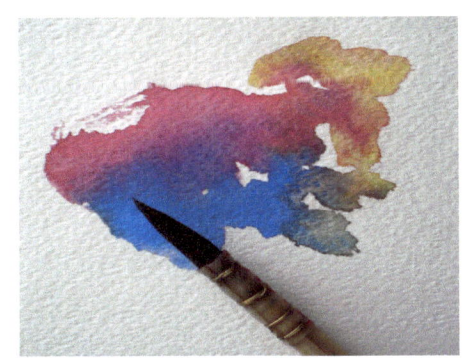

The drag stroke is made with a mop brush. Mop held horizontal to the paper and drag across the paper by the fat part of the brush. The faster

movement across the paper the brush will skip more area of white paper. This is a wonderful technique that will add spark to your painting.

The Mop brush has a nice point when wet. With light pressure the point will get into small places.

Then press down to spread the hair and discharge most of the water.

Notes and Ideas

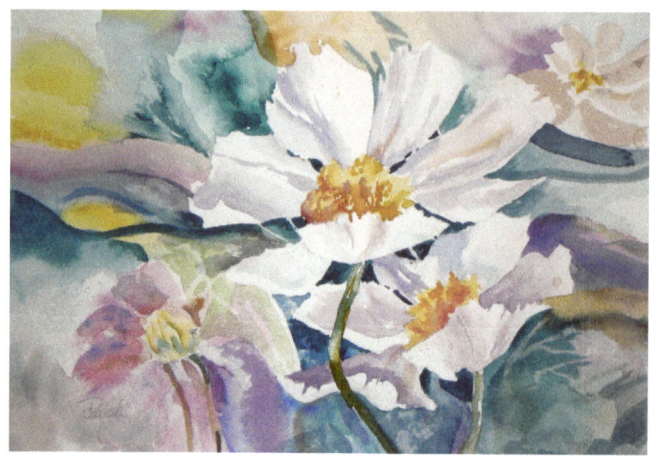

7

Just Do It! Tips and Brush Care

Tips:

* The watercolor brush is the most important tool for creating your visual story.

* The flow of water and leaving bits of white paper is a challenge.

* The combination of Transparent Watercolor and white paper gives watercolor its luminosity, clarity, and eye-catching beauty.

* Stand at the easel to paint. Extend your arm to place a stroke on paper. This allows freedom of arm movement. At first, this might be intimidating, push through that hesitation and enjoy the magic of a spontaneous brushstroke.

* Gently hold the brush at the end of handle. Painting with watercolor takes a delicate touch. The brushes are light in our hand, the paint is watery and easy to apply, and the paper can handle washes and texturing. Gentle action does it!

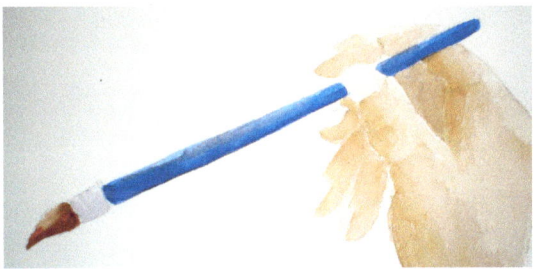

* Each brush is crafted to paint a specific stroke

Your Job: practice brush strokes and push to its limits by adding your personality and flair. Just like a signature, everyone has a distinct mark on paper.

My Job: introduce brush strokes and how to care for your brushes. Remember, water is the key to placing color on paper.

Water in Brush:

Wet ~ Damp ~ Dry

a. **Wet Brush ~ Sopping,** holds maximum amount of water.

b. **Damp Brush ~ Workable,** some water removed

c. **Dry Brush ~ Thirsty Brush**, ready to pick-up puddles of water or lay in color that doesn't move on the page.

Hint: Always have your brush hair wet before loading your brush with color.

Brush and Paper painting process:

Wet Paper/ **Wet** Brush

Wet Paper/**Dry** Brush

Dry Paper/**Wet** Brush

Dry Paper/**Dry** Brush

- Talking about a dry brush stroke doesn't mean work with dry brush hairs. Dry brush stroke is the name of a technique, meaning the brush is damp or has a small amount of water in it.

- Always put your brush hair in water before you pick up paint. Always rinse your brush after use. Any color dried in the furl will release the next time the brush is wet. The stored color and the color you picked up will discharge together, oops! Might not be the color mix you want!

Brush Care

Very simple, water is the key to painting and cleaning your brush.

- Swish brush in water container to wash out paint residue.
- Touch paper towel or sponge to absorb water from brush hair.
- Lay brush on table to dry. When dry, stand with brush hair up in jar or place in brush holder for safekeeping.

Your brushes can last for many years if you take the time to clean and store properly.

The illustration below shows how to load the brush with paint and bring to mixing area. **Let's practice!**

Wet ~ Sponge ~ Load ~ Mix

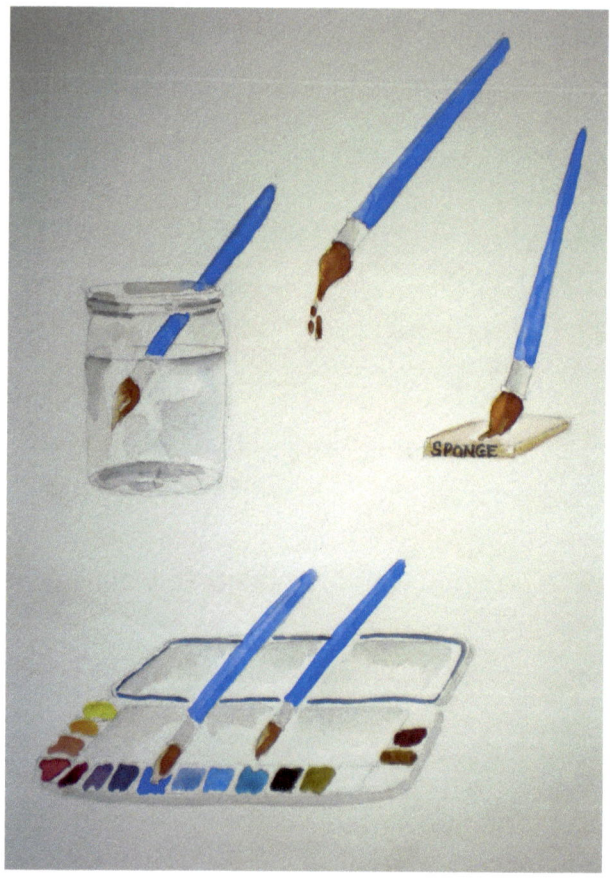

Process to bring paint to paper

1. Rinse to wet brush.
2. Loaded Brush, full of water
3. Blot Brush on sponge to control amount of water
4. Pick-Up paint from paint wells
5. Bring to open mixing area
6. Add water to adjust color value, and then bring to paper.

Notes and Ideas

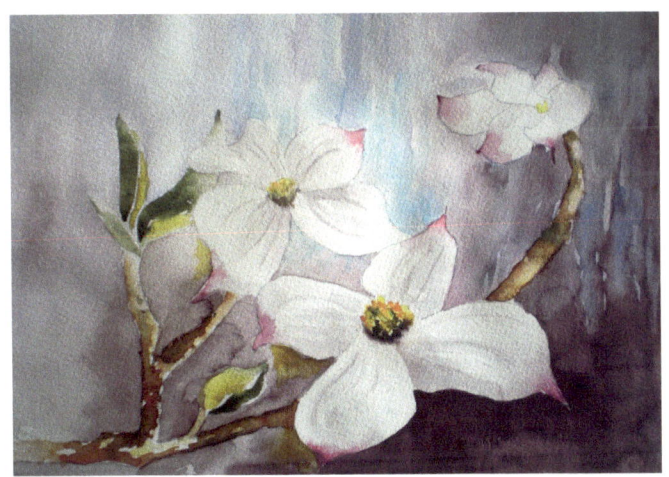

8

Demonstration

Paint along with me, no pressure, just start with loading the brush, hold at end of handle, and follow along with the demonstration.

In this demonstration I will use all five brushes. Round, Flat, Rigger, Fan, and Mop.

Using these colors: Earthen Green, Cerulean Blue, Purple, Burnt Sienna, and New Gamboge.

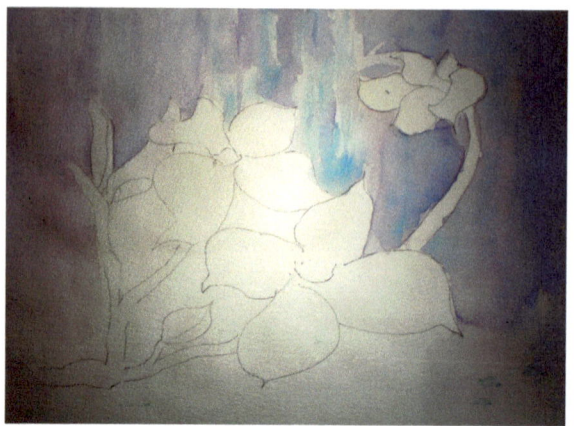

Pencil Sketch

I sketched in the outside line of the flowers and stems, to establish the placement for the center of interest.

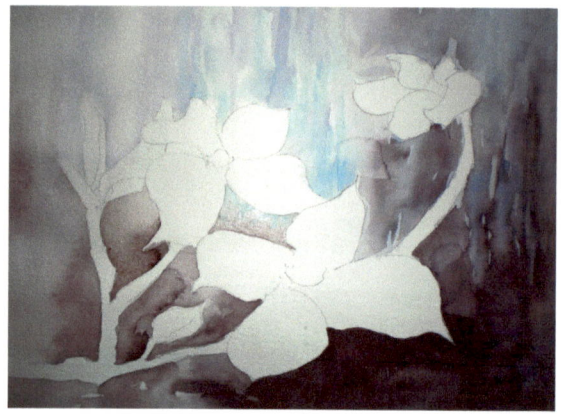

Use Mop Brush to wet light value background. Notice the vertical stroke using light purple (water added to lighten color) and cerulean blue. Wet into

Wet allows the color to mingle and merge with no hard edge.

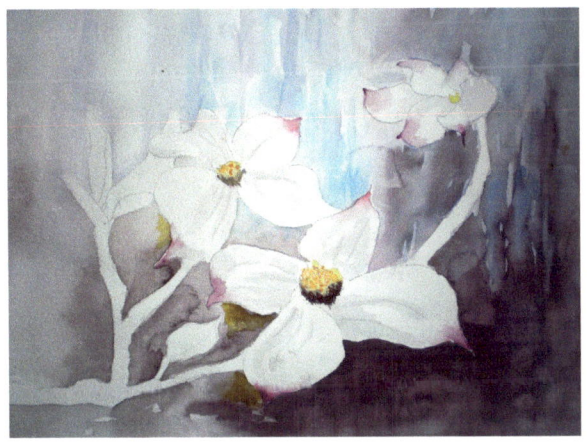

Use Round #8 Brush for flower tips.

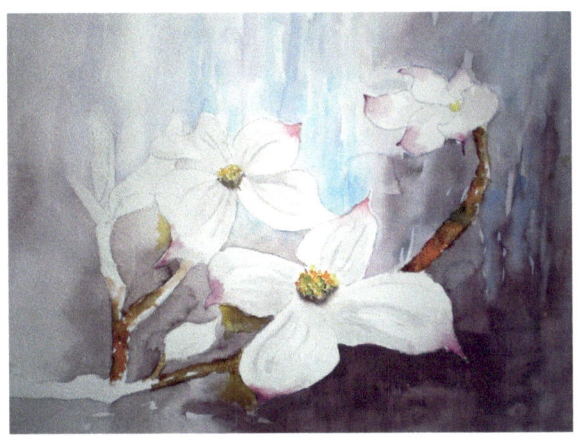

Used 3/4 " flat brush for stems.

Paint lower right in a darker value of Burnt Sienna and Purple to make grayed purple. Notice this is not a wash, but a textured look. This technique, gives the impression that something is going on in the background. Add light value purple to shade and give the illusion of lift.

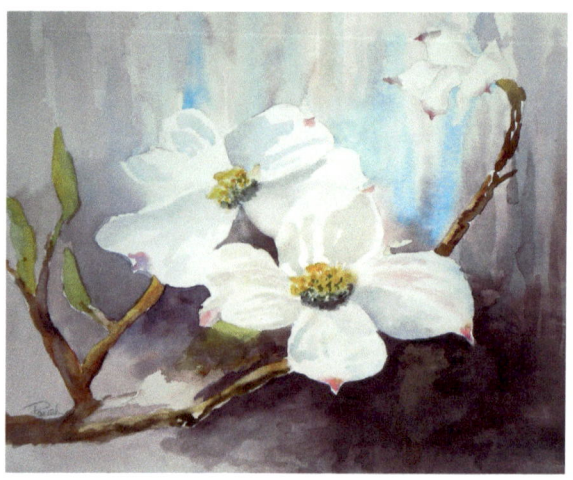

Paint the two toned tips of the blossom. Use Permanent Rose on the end of petal and Alizarin Crimson on the tip.

Burnt Sienna and Ultra Marine Blue mingle and merge on stem. Adds interest with stem color change. Use #8 Round Brush

Leave some white paper to light up the branch.

Paint the center with yellow, before it dries, use tip of brush to drop in the green.

Use #8 round brush add Yellow Green to one side of leaf, the other add Earthen Green

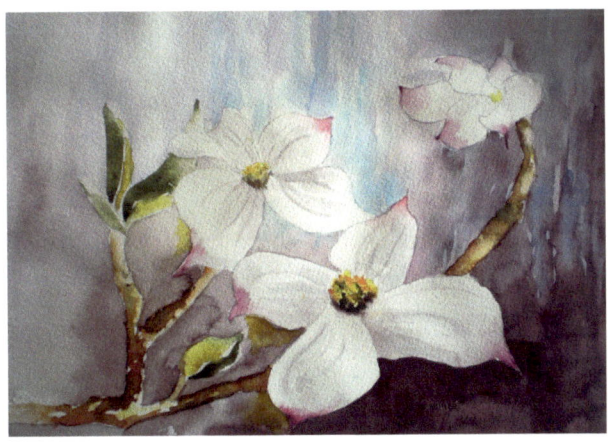

Use the Rigger or Fan Brush to add lines on petals.

Round #8, paint the leaves and stem. Use light green and dark green to add form to the leaf. Finish off the stem with New Gamboge and Burnt Sienna. Do not mix the colors place them side-by-side. Remember you are practicing with your watercolor brush. The purpose of this exercise is to become comfortable with a brush in your hand, loading the brush with color, and placing watercolor on the paper, this is your goal.

Learning is a Step-by-Step process

Consistency will build a solid foundation of knowledge

Practice and have fun, this painting process will become second nature.

Notes and Ideas

Here are a few of my thoughts on painting!

* Painting is a learned skill!

It takes practice to learn the painting process.

* It takes courage to paint!

Brush in hand, marks on paper for all to see.

* Good for your Soul!

Focus ~ Make Decisions ~ Play

* Style

Painters develop a painting style as unique as their handwriting!

* Personality

Like handwriting, no one has the same touch.

* Find a painting tribe!

Other artists to paint with, safety in numbers!

Artist/Teacher/Author

Barbara A Parish

 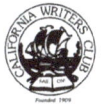 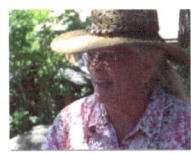

www.barbaraparish.weebly.com

barbaraparish@verizon.net

My enthusiasm and desire to paint with watercolor is unstoppable. From the time I picked up a paintbrush in 1988 until now, I've been hooked on the discovery of brush strokes.

I paint on location to familiarize myself with the landscape. My ride is a CJ-5 Jeep. I explore the back roads of the High Desert and mountain area near my Hesperia Studio. Being on location allows me to get emotionally evolved with the landscape. I can SEE the warm or cool temperature in color and enjoy the long shadows that cast over the ground in early morning and late afternoon.

My home-based studio is my comfort zone. I enjoy

the soft sounds of American Indian Flute and Drum music playing in the background, while I paint. My easel stands tall so I can walk up to it and paint. Standing while painting gives me freedom to step away from the easel to SEE what's happening on the paper.

My interest in painting extends beyond practice; I teach watercolor brush techniques and the courage to paint in a weekly class, exhibit my paintings in outdoor shows, and enter gallery competition.

Born in Chicago, raised in California, I consider myself a true Southern California gal. I enjoy the sunny days, open spaces, and easy travel to the mountains and the sea.   My car is loaded with painting supplies, my rolling studio.

Affiliations:

 **Women Artists of the West**, WAOW

Signature and Emeritus Member

Editor: The West Wind, The Voice of WAOW

* Cactus Flower received the Sycan Band of

Kumeyaay Nation Award.

* WAOW granted me the Lynn Thomas Scholarship
Award to advance my art career.

Plein Air Artists of Riverside, my painting
tribe.

**California Writers Club ~ High Desert
Branch**, my writing tribe.

Notes and Ideas

Desire ~ Tenacity ~ Personality ~ Practice

www.ingramcontent.com/pod-product-compliance
Lightning Source LLC
Chambersburg PA
CBHW040908180526
45159CB00010BA/2971